The In and Outs of Sex

A Comprehensive Guide for Young Men

Kelly Anderson

Table Of Contents

Chapter 1: Understanding Your Body

The Male Anatomy

and "Men's health".

The Male Anatomy

As a young adult man, it is important to have a good understanding of your own anatomy. The male anatomy is complex and fascinating, and it plays a crucial role in your sexual health and overall well-being. In this section, we will explore the different parts of the male anatomy and their functions.

The Penis

The penis is the primary sexual organ of the male body. It is made up of three main parts: the root, the shaft, and the glans. The root of the penis is the base, where it attaches to the pelvic bone. The shaft is the long, cylindrical part of the penis that extends from the root to the glans. The glans is the rounded head of the penis.

The penis contains two main chambers called the corpora cavernosa, which fill with blood during an erection. The urethra, which is the channel that carries urine and semen out of the body, runs through the center of the penis.

The Testicles

The testicles, also known as the testes, are two small, egg-shaped organs located in the scrotum. The scrotum is a sac of skin that hangs beneath the penis, and it helps to regulate the temperature of the testicles. The testicles are responsible for producing testosterone, the male sex hormone, and sperm.

The Prostate Gland

The prostate gland is a small, walnut-shaped gland located just below the bladder. It is an important part of the male reproductive system, as it produces seminal fluid, which is a component of semen. The prostate gland can be felt during a rectal exam, and it can become enlarged or inflamed, which can cause problems with urination and sexual function.

Understanding your own anatomy is an important part of maintaining good sexual health and overall well-being. By taking the time to learn about the different parts of your body and how they function, you can be better prepared to take care of yourself and enjoy a healthy and fulfilling sex life.

Hormones and Their Function

Hormones are the chemical messengers that regulate various bodily functions, including sexual development and behavior. In this subchapter, we will explore the different hormones present in the male body and their functions.

Testosterone is the most well-known hormone associated with male sexuality. It is responsible for the development of male sex organs, such as the penis and testicles, as well as secondary sexual characteristics like body hair and deepening of the voice. Testosterone also plays a crucial role in sperm production and sex drive.

Another hormone that is important for male sexual health is estrogen. Yes, you read that right – men have estrogen too! In fact, it is necessary for maintaining healthy bones and cardiovascular health. However, having too much estrogen can lead to unwanted side effects like gynecomastia (enlargement of breast tissue) and decreased sex drive.

Progesterone is a hormone mostly associated with female reproductive health, but it is also present in men. It helps regulate the menstrual cycle in women and contributes to the development of sperm in men.

Lastly, oxytocin is often referred to as the "love hormone" because it is released during sexual activity, childbirth, and breastfeeding. It creates feelings of intimacy and bonding between partners, and also contributes to orgasm and ejaculation in men.

It is important to understand how these hormones work in order to maintain optimal sexual health. Hormonal imbalances can lead to a variety of issues, including erectile dysfunction, low sex drive, and infertility. If you suspect that you may have a hormonal imbalance, it is crucial to speak with a healthcare professional.

In conclusion, hormones play a vital role in male sexual health. Testosterone, estrogen, progesterone, and oxytocin all contribute to different aspects of sexual development and behavior. Understanding how these hormones work can help you maintain a healthy and fulfilling sex life.

Sexual Response Cycle

The Sexual Response Cycle: A Comprehensive Guide for Young Men

Sexual arousal is a natural and healthy part of human sexuality. The Sexual Response Cycle is a physiological process that describes the stages of sexual response in both men and women. Understanding this process is crucial for young men who want to have a healthy and enjoyable sex life.

The Sexual Response Cycle has four stages: excitement, plateau, orgasm, and resolution. These stages occur in both men and women, but the timing and intensity of each stage can vary from person to person.

Excitement: This stage is characterized by increased blood flow to the genitals, resulting in erection in men and vaginal lubrication in women. Breathing and heart rate increase, and the skin may flush. Arousal can be triggered by physical stimulation, visual or auditory cues, or mental fantasies.

Plateau: During this stage, sexual tension builds and physical changes peak. The penis becomes fully erect, and the testicles move closer to the body. In women, the clitoris may become more sensitive, and the nipples may become erect. This stage can last from a few seconds to several minutes.

Orgasm: This is the climax of sexual arousal, characterized by intense physical and emotional pleasure. In men, orgasm is usually accompanied by ejaculation. In women, orgasm can be achieved through stimulation of the clitoris or vaginal walls.

Resolution: After orgasm, the body returns to its normal state. The penis becomes flaccid, and the testicles return to their normal position. In women, the clitoris and vagina return to their pre-arousal state. This stage can last from a few minutes to several hours.

It's important to note that the Sexual Response Cycle is not always linear and can be influenced by a variety of factors, including stress, anxiety, medication, and relationship issues. Communicating with sexual partners and understanding each other's needs and desires can help enhance sexual pleasure and satisfaction.

In conclusion, understanding the Sexual Response Cycle is crucial for young men who want to have a healthy and enjoyable sex life. By being aware of the stages of sexual response and communicating with sexual partners, young men can enhance their sexual pleasure and satisfaction.

Chapter 2: Communicating About Sex

Consent and Boundaries

Consent and Boundaries: A Crucial Aspect of Healthy and Respectful Sexual Relationships

Consent and boundaries are two essential concepts that young men must understand to ensure that their sexual interactions are healthy and respectful. Consent refers to the explicit and enthusiastic agreement between two individuals to engage in sexual activity. Boundaries, on the other hand, are the limits that individuals set regarding what they are comfortable with in sexual and intimate situations.

It is crucial to understand that consent is not the mere absence of a "no." Instead, it is an active and ongoing process that requires clear communication and the absence of coercion or pressure. Consent can be withdrawn at any time, and it is essential to respect this decision if it is made. Young men must learn to recognize when their partner is comfortable and enthusiastic about engaging in sexual activity and when they are not. Being respectful of boundaries and ensuring that both partners are comfortable and consensual will lead to a pleasurable sexual experience for both parties.

It is also important to note that boundaries are not just physical but can also be emotional and psychological. Young men must learn to recognize and respect their partner's boundaries, whether they are related to physical touch or emotional intimacy. Communication is key in establishing boundaries, and it is essential to have an open and honest conversation about what each partner is comfortable with before engaging in sexual activity.

Moreover, young men must understand that boundaries can change over time and that it is crucial to respect these changes. As individuals grow and evolve, their boundaries may change, and it is essential to communicate and adjust accordingly. It is also crucial to recognize that boundaries may differ from person to person, and it is essential to respect and honor each individual's unique boundaries.

In conclusion, understanding consent and boundaries is crucial to ensuring healthy and respectful sexual relationships. Young men must learn to communicate openly and honestly with their partners and respect each other's boundaries. By doing so, they can ensure that their sexual experiences are safe, enjoyable, and mutually consensual.

Effective Communication in Sexual Relationships

Effective Communication in Sexual Relationships

Sexual relationships can be a tricky subject to navigate, especially when it comes to communication. However, effective communication is essential to building a healthy and fulfilling sexual relationship. Here are some tips on how to communicate effectively with your partner:

1. Be Open and Honest

One of the most important aspects of effective communication in a sexual relationship is being open and honest. This means being willing to talk about your desires, needs, and boundaries with your partner. It can be difficult to initiate these conversations, but they are crucial to building a healthy sexual relationship.

2. Listen to Your Partner

Effective communication is a two-way street. It's not just about expressing your own needs and desires, but also about listening to your partner. Make sure to actively listen and ask questions to ensure that you understand their perspective.

3. Use "I" Statements

When discussing sensitive topics, such as sexual desires or boundaries, it's important to use "I" statements instead of "you" statements. This helps to avoid placing blame or making the other person feel defensive. For example, instead of saying "You never do what I want in bed," try saying "I would really like to try something new in bed."

4. Be Respectful

Respect is key in any relationship, including a sexual one. Make sure to communicate in a way that is respectful of your partner's feelings and boundaries. Avoid making assumptions or pressuring them into doing something they are not comfortable with.

5. Practice Active Consent

Consent is an essential part of any sexual relationship. Make sure to communicate clearly and actively seek consent before engaging in any sexual activity. This means asking for permission, respecting your partner's answer, and checking in throughout the experience.

In conclusion, effective communication is crucial to building a healthy and fulfilling sexual relationship. By being open and honest, listening to your partner, using "I" statements, being respectful, and practicing active consent, you can create a safe and enjoyable sexual experience for both you and your partner.

Common Misconceptions About Sex

Common Misconceptions About Sex

Sex is a complex and multifaceted topic that is often subject to a range of misconceptions and myths. As a young adult man, you may have already encountered some of these false beliefs, either through peers, media, or other sources. In this section, we aim to dispel some of the most common misconceptions about sex and provide you with accurate and factual information.

Misconception #1: Sex is only about pleasure.

While pleasure is certainly a significant aspect of sex, it is not the only one. Sex can also be about intimacy, connection, and even reproduction. It is important to understand that sex involves two (or more) people, and that their needs, desires, and boundaries should be respected and considered.

Misconception #2: Women always orgasm during sex.

This is a common myth perpetuated by media and pornography. In reality, many women do not experience orgasm during intercourse alone, and may require additional stimulation or different techniques to achieve it. Communication, experimentation, and patience are key to ensuring that both partners enjoy their sexual experiences.

Misconception #3: Men are always ready for sex.

Men's sexual desire and ability can vary depending on a range of factors, including stress, fatigue, medication, and emotional state. It is important to recognize that men are not always in the mood for sex and that their consent should always be obtained before engaging in any sexual activity.

Misconception #4: Condoms reduce pleasure.

While some men may report decreased sensitivity or discomfort when using condoms, this is not the case for everyone. In fact, condoms can provide a range of benefits, including protection against sexually transmitted infections and unwanted pregnancies. It is important to explore different types and brands of condoms to find the one that works best for you.

Misconception #5: Masturbation is harmful or shameful.

Masturbation is a natural and healthy aspect of sexuality that can provide pleasure, stress relief, and self-exploration. It is important to understand that there is no shame or harm in masturbation, and that it can even have positive effects on mental and physical health.

In conclusion, it is essential to question and challenge common misconceptions about sex to ensure that you have accurate and factual information. By understanding the complexities and nuances of sexuality, you can have more fulfilling and satisfying sexual experiences, and build healthy and respectful relationships with your partners.

Chapter 3: STIs and Safe Sex Practices

Understanding STIs and Their Transmission

and "Health education".

Sexually transmitted infections (STIs) are infections that are spread through sexual contact. These infections can be caused by bacteria, viruses, or parasites and can affect both men and women. Understanding STIs and their transmission is important for young adult men as it can help them protect themselves and their partners from these infections.

STIs can be transmitted through vaginal, anal, or oral sex. The most common STIs include chlamydia, gonorrhea, syphilis, herpes, human papillomavirus (HPV), and human immunodeficiency virus (HIV). Some STIs can be cured with antibiotics while others cannot be cured and can only be managed with medication.

It is important to note that STIs can be present even if there are no symptoms. This means that a person can have an STI and not know it, which can lead to the infection being unknowingly spread to others. That is why it is important to get tested for STIs regularly, especially if you are sexually active with multiple partners.

Using condoms during sexual activity is one of the most effective ways to prevent the transmission of STIs. It is important to use condoms correctly and consistently every time you have sex. It is also important to use condoms during oral sex as some STIs can be transmitted this way as well.

It is also important to communicate with your sexual partners about their sexual health and history. If you or your partner have been diagnosed with an STI, it is important to get treated and to avoid sexual activity until the infection has cleared.

In conclusion, understanding STIs and their transmission is crucial for young adult men who are sexually active. Regular testing, proper condom use, and open communication with sexual partners can help prevent the spread of STIs and promote sexual health and well-being.

Preventing STIs: Condoms, Testing, and Vaccines

STIs (Sexually Transmitted Infections) are a serious matter that can affect anyone who engages in sexual activity. These infections can cause a range of health problems, from mild irritation to long-term complications. Fortunately, there are several ways that you can protect yourself from STIs.

One of the most effective methods of preventing STIs is through the use of condoms. Condoms act as a barrier, preventing the exchange of bodily fluids during sexual activity. When used correctly, condoms provide an excellent level of protection against STIs. It is important to use a new condom every time you engage in sexual activity, as condoms can break or become damaged during use.

Another way to prevent STIs is through regular testing. STIs can often be asymptomatic, meaning that you may not show any signs of infection. Regular testing can ensure that you are aware of any potential infections and can seek treatment if necessary. Testing is particularly important if you engage in sexual activity with multiple partners.

Vaccines are another effective method of preventing some STIs. The HPV (Human Papillomavirus) vaccine is recommended for both males and females, as it can prevent several types of cancers and genital warts. The Hepatitis B vaccine is also recommended for those who are at risk of contracting the virus.

It is important to be open and honest with your sexual partners about STIs. If you have an infection, it is important to inform your partner so that they can seek treatment and prevent the spread of the infection. It is also important to practice safe sex, even if you or your partner have been tested and are infection-free.

In summary, preventing STIs requires a combination of methods. Condoms provide excellent protection, regular testing can identify infections, and vaccines can prevent some infections altogether. It is important to be open and honest with your sexual partners and to practice safe sex to protect yourself and others from STIs.

How to Talk About STIs with Partners

and "Sexual health".

Talking about sexually transmitted infections (STIs) can be a daunting task, but it's an essential conversation to have with your partner(s). STIs are common, and they can have serious consequences if left untreated. Here are some tips on how to talk about STIs with your partners.

1. Know your stuff.

Before talking to your partner(s) about STIs, make sure you have a good understanding of the topic. You should know how STIs are transmitted, what the symptoms are, and how they can be treated. You can find reliable information on the internet, or you can speak to a healthcare professional.

2. Set the mood.

Choose a time and place where you can talk openly and comfortably. This might be after dinner, in bed, or during a walk. Make sure you and your partner(s) are relaxed and not distracted.

3. Be honest.

Tell your partner(s) that you want to talk about STIs because you care about their health and safety, as well as your own. Be honest about your sexual history, including any past STIs you may have had. If you haven't been tested recently, suggest that you both get tested before having sex.

4. Be respectful.

Talking about STIs can be a sensitive topic, so it's important to be respectful of your partner(s) and their feelings. Avoid using judgmental language or making assumptions about their sexual history. Listen to their concerns and answer their questions honestly.

5. Be proactive.

Once you've had the conversation about STIs, make sure you take steps to protect yourself and your partner(s). Use condoms or other barrier methods during sex, and get tested regularly if you're sexually active. Remember, prevention is key.

In conclusion, talking about STIs with your partner(s) is an important part of being sexually responsible. By being informed, honest, respectful, and proactive, you can help prevent the spread of STIs and protect your health and the health of your partner(s).

Chapter 4: Masturbation and Sexual Exploration

Benefits of Masturbation

and "Men's health".

Masturbation is a completely natural and healthy activity that is often stigmatized and misunderstood. In reality, there are numerous benefits to indulging in regular self-pleasure. Here are just a few:

1. Stress relief: Masturbation is a great way to relieve stress and tension. It releases endorphins which can provide a sense of relaxation and well-being.

2. Better sleep: Many people report falling asleep faster and sleeping more soundly after masturbating. This is likely due to the same endorphins that provide stress relief.

3. Improved sexual function: Masturbation can help you become more familiar with your body and what feels good. This knowledge can translate into better sexual experiences with partners.

4. Prostate health: Regular ejaculation, whether through masturbation or sex, can help keep the prostate healthy and reduce the risk of prostate cancer.

5. Mood booster: Masturbation can release dopamine, a neurotransmitter associated with pleasure and reward. This can improve your mood and overall sense of well-being.

6. Sexual release without risk of STIs or pregnancy: Masturbation is a safe and convenient way to experience sexual pleasure without the risk of sexually transmitted infections or unwanted pregnancy.

7. Improved self-esteem: Masturbation can help you feel more comfortable and confident with your body and your sexuality. This can lead to improved self-esteem and body image.

It's important to remember that masturbation is a personal choice and there is no right or wrong frequency or method. As long as it is done in a safe and consensual manner, there is no harm in exploring your own sexuality through masturbation.

Techniques for Masturbation

Masturbation is a natural and healthy way to explore your own body and learn what feels good to you. It's also a great way to relieve stress and tension. However, not everyone knows the best techniques for self-pleasure. In this chapter, we'll explore some tried-and-true techniques for masturbation.

1. Use Lubrication

Using lubrication during masturbation can make the experience more pleasurable and prevent discomfort or irritation. You can use water-based lubricants like KY Jelly or silicone-based lubricants like Astroglide. Avoid oil-based lubricants like baby oil or petroleum jelly, as they can damage condoms and cause infections.

2. Experiment with Different Strokes

There are many different ways to stroke your penis, so don't be afraid to experiment and find what feels best for you. Some popular techniques include the up-and-down stroke, the circular stroke, and the twisting stroke. You can also try using different pressures and speeds to vary the sensation.

3. Use Sex Toys

Sex toys can add a new dimension to your masturbation routine. You can try using a vibrator or a prostate massager to stimulate different areas of your body. Just make sure to clean your toys thoroughly after use.

4. Try Edging

Edging involves bringing yourself to the brink of orgasm and then backing off before you climax. This can make your eventual orgasm more intense and satisfying. To try edging, masturbate as usual until you feel yourself getting close to orgasm. Then, stop or slow down the stimulation until you feel yourself becoming less aroused. Repeat this process several times before allowing yourself to orgasm.

5. Use Visualization

Fantasizing or visualizing can add an extra layer of stimulation to your masturbation routine. You can imagine a sexy scenario or recall a past sexual experience. Just make sure that your fantasies are consensual and respectful.

Remember, there is no right or wrong way to masturbate. The most important thing is to listen to your body and do what feels good to you. Happy exploring!

Exploring Sexual Fantasies

and "Sexual exploration."

Exploring Sexual Fantasies

Sexual fantasies are a normal part of human sexuality. They can range from mild to wild, and can be a great way to explore your desires and turn-ons. While some people may feel shy or embarrassed about their fantasies, it's important to remember that they are a natural part of sexual expression. In this chapter, we will explore the different types of sexual fantasies and how to safely explore them.

Types of Sexual Fantasies

There are many different types of sexual fantasies, but some of the most common include:

1. Power Play: This type of fantasy involves a power dynamic between two people, such as a dominant and submissive role.

2. Taboo: Taboo fantasies involve sexual acts that are considered socially unacceptable, such as incest, rape, or voyeurism.

3. Fetish: A fetish is a specific object or body part that someone is sexually attracted to, such as feet, leather, or latex.

4. Group Sex: This type of fantasy involves multiple partners, often in a group setting.

5. Same-Sex Fantasies: These fantasies involve exploring same-sex attraction or experiences.

Exploring Your Fantasies

If you're interested in exploring your sexual fantasies, there are a few things to keep in mind:

1. Consent: Consent is key when it comes to exploring sexual fantasies. Make sure that any partners involved are fully aware of your desires and are comfortable with them.

2. Communication: It's important to communicate with your partner(s) about your fantasies and what you're comfortable with. This can help ensure that everyone is on the same page and that boundaries are respected.

3. Safety: Always prioritize safety when exploring sexual fantasies. This can include using protection, setting boundaries, and having a safe word in case things become too intense.

4. Fantasies vs. Reality: It's important to remember that sexual fantasies are not always a reflection of what you want in real life. Some fantasies may be better left as just that – fantasies.

In conclusion, sexual fantasies can be a fun and exciting way to explore your desires and turn-ons. Just remember to prioritize consent, communication, safety, and the distinction between fantasy and reality. Happy exploring!

Chapter 5: Sexual Intercourse

Preparing for Sexual Intercourse

Preparing for Sexual Intercourse

Sexual intercourse is an important aspect of human life, and it is essential that you are well prepared for it. While some people may view sex as a spontaneous act, it is important to note that it requires preparation and planning. This chapter will provide you with some important tips on how to prepare for sexual intercourse.

1. Communicate with your partner

Before engaging in sexual intercourse, it is important to communicate with your partner. Discuss your expectations, boundaries, and desires. Make sure that you both agree on what you want and what you are comfortable with. This can help to ensure that both partners have a positive and enjoyable experience.

2. Practice safe sex

Sexually transmitted infections (STIs) are a common problem among sexually active individuals. Therefore, it is important to practice safe sex to avoid the risk of contracting an STI. Use a condom during sexual intercourse to reduce the risk of STI transmission.

3. Use lubrication

Lubrication can help to reduce friction during sexual intercourse, which can make it more enjoyable for both partners. It is important to use a water-based lubricant, as oil-based lubricants can damage condoms and increase the risk of STI transmission.

4. Prepare your body

It is important to prepare your body for sexual intercourse. This includes grooming your genital area, practicing good hygiene, and avoiding foods that can cause bad breath or body odor. Additionally, it is important to use the bathroom before engaging in sexual intercourse to avoid any discomfort or embarrassment.

5. Relax

Sexual intercourse can be a stressful experience for some people. Therefore, it is important to relax and make sure that you are comfortable. Take deep breaths, listen to calming music, or engage in other relaxation techniques to help calm your nerves.

In conclusion, preparing for sexual intercourse is essential for a positive and enjoyable experience. Communication with your partner, practicing safe sex, using lubrication, preparing your body, and relaxing are all important factors to consider when preparing for sexual intercourse. Remember to always prioritize your safety and the safety of your partner.

Techniques for Pleasurable Intercourse

and "Sexual health".

Techniques for Pleasurable Intercourse

Sex is a wonderful experience that can be enjoyed by both partners if done properly. However, many young men struggle with achieving pleasurable intercourse due to a lack of knowledge, experience, or confidence. Fear not, as there are several techniques that can help you achieve a more satisfying sexual experience.

Foreplay: Foreplay is a crucial part of sexual intercourse as it helps to increase arousal and lubrication, making penetration easier and more enjoyable. Engaging in foreplay can involve kissing, touching, or oral sex. Take the time to explore your partner's body and learn what they like and dislike. This will not only help you to please them but also help you to better understand your own preferences.

Communication: Communication is key when it comes to pleasurable intercourse. Be open and honest about your desires, needs, and concerns. Ask your partner what they like and what they do not like. This will allow you both to explore each other's bodies and find what works best for you.

Positioning: The position you choose can greatly affect your level of pleasure during intercourse. Experiment with different positions to find what works best for you and your partner. Some popular positions include missionary, doggy style, and cowgirl. Remember that not all positions work for everyone, so be open to trying new things.

Stimulation: Stimulation of the clitoris or G-spot can greatly increase pleasure during intercourse. Take the time to explore these areas with your partner and find what works best for them. You can use your fingers or a sex toy to stimulate these areas.

Relaxation: It is important to be relaxed and comfortable during intercourse. Stress and anxiety can make it difficult to achieve a satisfying sexual experience. Take the time to set the mood with candles, music, or other relaxing techniques. Focus on your partner and the moment, allowing yourself to fully enjoy the experience.

In conclusion, achieving pleasurable intercourse requires open communication, experimentation, and a willingness to explore your partner's body. Take the time to learn what works best for both you and your partner, and remember that everyone is different. With practice and patience, you can achieve a more satisfying and enjoyable sexual experience.

Sexual Problems and Solutions

and "Men's health".

Sexual Problems and Solutions

Sexual problems are a common issue that many young adult men face. These problems can arise due to various factors such as stress, anxiety, depression, relationship issues, medical conditions, and lifestyle choices. However, the good news is that most sexual problems can be treated or managed with the right solutions.

Erectile Dysfunction (ED)

ED is a condition where a man has difficulty achieving or maintaining an erection during sexual activity. This can be caused by physical or psychological factors such as diabetes, high blood pressure, anxiety, and depression. The solutions to ED include medication, lifestyle changes such as exercise and quitting smoking, and therapy.

Premature Ejaculation (PE)

PE is a condition where a man ejaculates sooner than he or his partner would like during sexual activity. This can be caused by psychological factors such as anxiety, stress, and depression. The solutions to PE include medication, pelvic floor exercises, and therapy.

Low Libido

Low libido is a condition where a man has a reduced interest in sexual activity. This can be caused by physical or psychological factors such as low testosterone levels, stress, and depression. The solutions to low libido include medication, lifestyle changes such as exercise and a healthy diet, and therapy.

Sexually Transmitted Infections (STIs)

STIs are infections that are spread through sexual contact. They can cause various symptoms such as pain, discharge, and itching. The solutions to STIs include practicing safe sex by using condoms, getting tested regularly, and receiving treatment if necessary.

In conclusion, sexual problems are common among young adult men, but they can be treated or managed with the right solutions. It's important to seek help from a healthcare provider if you are experiencing any sexual problems. Remember, taking care of your sexual health is an important part of maintaining overall health and well-being.

Chapter 6: Relationships and Sex

Navigating Sexual Relationships

Navigating Sexual Relationships

Sexual relationships can be a complicated and overwhelming experience for young adult men. There are several factors to consider, such as consent, communication, and sexual health. It is essential to understand these factors to ensure a healthy and positive sexual experience.

Consent is the foundation of any sexual relationship. Both parties should explicitly agree to engage in sexual activity. Consent is not just about saying yes or no; it is about respecting boundaries and understanding that consent can be revoked at any time. If your partner seems uncomfortable or hesitant, it is best to stop and ask if they are okay. Remember, no means no.

Communication is key to a healthy sexual relationship. It is essential to communicate openly and honestly with your partner about your likes and dislikes, boundaries, and expectations. This can help avoid misunderstandings and ensure that both parties are satisfied with the experience.

Sexual health is also a crucial aspect of any sexual relationship. It is essential to practice safe sex by using condoms or other forms of contraception to prevent unwanted pregnancies and sexually transmitted infections. Regular testing for STIs is also recommended, especially if you have multiple sexual partners.

It is also important to understand the different types of sexual relationships. Casual hookups and one-night stands may not be for everyone, and it is okay to say no to these types of encounters. It is essential to be honest with yourself and your partner about your intentions and expectations.

In conclusion, navigating sexual relationships can be challenging, but it is essential to prioritize consent, communication, and sexual health. Be respectful of your partner's boundaries and communicate openly and honestly. Remember, a healthy sexual relationship should be enjoyable and safe for both parties.

Long-Distance Relationships and Sexual Intimacy

and "Relationships".

Long-distance relationships can be challenging, but when it comes to sexual intimacy, the distance can make it even more difficult. However, with communication, trust, and creativity, long-distance couples can maintain a healthy and fulfilling sexual relationship.

Communication is key in any relationship, but it is especially important in long-distance relationships. Talk openly and honestly about your sexual needs and desires. Discuss what you enjoy and what makes you feel uncomfortable. Share your fantasies with each other and explore ways to make them a reality, even when you're apart.

Trust is also crucial in a long-distance relationship. Make sure you are both on the same page when it comes to the boundaries of your sexual relationship. It is important to establish trust and respect for each other's boundaries, and to respect each other's privacy.

Creativity is essential when it comes to maintaining sexual intimacy in a long-distance relationship. Use technology to your advantage. Video chat, sexting, and phone sex can all be great ways to stay connected and satisfy each other's sexual needs. Send each other naughty messages and pictures to keep the sexual tension alive.

It is important to remember that a long-distance relationship is not just about the sexual aspect. It is important to maintain emotional intimacy as well. Share your thoughts, feelings, and experiences with each other. Plan visits and make the most of the time you have together. Remember that physical intimacy is just one aspect of a healthy and fulfilling relationship.

In conclusion, long-distance relationships can be challenging, but with communication, trust, and creativity, it is possible to maintain a healthy and fulfilling sexual relationship. Remember to prioritize emotional intimacy as well, and make the most of the time you have together. With commitment and effort, long-distance relationships can be just as satisfying as any other relationship.

Dealing with Breakups and Heartbreak

Dealing with Breakups and Heartbreak

Breakups and heartbreaks are an inevitable part of life, especially when it comes to relationships and dating. As a young adult man, it is important to understand how to deal with these situations in a healthy and productive manner.

The first step in dealing with a breakup is to allow yourself to feel the emotions that come with it. It is normal to feel sadness, anger, and confusion, and it is important to acknowledge and process these feelings. It can be helpful to talk to a trusted friend or family member, or even a therapist, to help you work through your emotions.

It is also important to take care of yourself during this time. Make sure to eat well, exercise, and get enough sleep. Engage in activities that make you happy and bring you joy, whether that be spending time with friends, pursuing a hobby, or simply taking some time to relax.

Avoid the temptation to turn to unhealthy coping mechanisms, such as alcohol or drugs, as these will only make the situation worse in the long run. Instead, focus on developing healthy coping mechanisms, such as meditation, journaling, or talking to a therapist.

Remember that time heals all wounds, and it is okay to take as much time as you need to heal. Avoid rushing into another relationship right away, as this can lead to more heartbreak and emotional turmoil.

If you find yourself struggling to move on, it may be helpful to seek professional help. A therapist can provide you with the tools and support you need to work through your emotions and move forward in a healthy way.

In conclusion, breakups and heartbreaks are a natural part of life, but they do not have to define you. By allowing yourself to feel your emotions, taking care of yourself, and seeking help when needed, you can move on from a breakup and emerge stronger and more resilient than ever before.

Chapter 7: Sex and Mental Health

Understanding the Connection Between Sex and Mental Health

and "Mental Health".

Understanding the Connection Between Sex and Mental Health

Sex is an integral part of human life and plays a significant role in our physical, emotional, and mental well-being. Research has shown that sex can have a positive impact on our mental health, but it can also have negative consequences if not approached with care and caution. In this chapter, we will explore the connection between sex and mental health and provide young men with the tools to navigate this important aspect of their lives.

Positive Effects of Sex on Mental Health

Sex can have a positive impact on our mental health in several ways. Firstly, it releases endorphins, which are feel-good hormones that reduce stress and anxiety and promote feelings of happiness and well-being. Secondly, sex fosters intimacy and connection with our partners, which can enhance our sense of belonging, security, and self-esteem. Thirdly, sex can improve our sleep quality, which is crucial for our mental health and overall well-being.

Negative Effects of Sex on Mental Health

While sex can have positive effects on our mental health, it can also have negative consequences if not approached with care and caution. Firstly, engaging in casual sex or having multiple sexual partners can increase the risk of contracting sexually transmitted infections (STIs) and unwanted pregnancies, which can cause stress, anxiety, and depression. Secondly, sex can be used as a coping mechanism for underlying mental health issues such as depression, anxiety, and trauma, which can perpetuate the cycle of negative emotions and behaviours. Lastly, sex addiction can lead to feelings of shame, guilt, and low self-esteem, which can have a detrimental effect on our mental health.

Tips for Navigating the Connection Between Sex and Mental Health

To ensure that sex has a positive impact on our mental health, it is important to approach it with care and caution. Firstly, practice safe sex by using protection and getting regular STI tests. Secondly, communicate openly and honestly with your partner about your sexual preferences, boundaries, and expectations. Thirdly, seek help if you are struggling with underlying mental health issues or sex addiction. Lastly, practice self-care by prioritizing your sleep, exercise, and healthy habits, which can enhance your mental health and overall well-being.

Conclusion

Sex is an important aspect of our lives that can have a significant impact on our mental health. By understanding the connection between sex and mental health and approaching it with care and caution, young men can ensure that sex has a positive impact on their mental health and overall well-being.

Common Mental Health Conditions and Sexual Functioning

and "Mental Health."

Mental health and sexual functioning are closely related, and it's essential to understand how one can affect the other. Mental health conditions can often cause sexual problems, which can impact a person's sexual satisfaction and overall well-being. In this chapter, we will discuss some common mental health conditions and their potential effects on sexual functioning.

Depression is a prevalent mental health condition that can cause a decrease in sexual desire, difficulty achieving orgasm, and erectile dysfunction. People with depression may also experience fatigue, which can make them less interested in sex. Anxiety is another common mental health condition that can affect sexual functioning. Anxiety can cause premature ejaculation, difficulty achieving or maintaining an erection, and a decrease in sexual desire.

Post-traumatic stress disorder (PTSD) is a mental health condition that can develop after a traumatic experience. People with PTSD may experience intrusive thoughts, nightmares, and flashbacks, making it difficult to feel safe and comfortable during sexual activity. PTSD can also cause a decrease in sexual desire and difficulty achieving orgasm.

Bipolar disorder is a mental health condition that causes extreme mood swings, from manic highs to depressive lows. During manic episodes, people with bipolar disorder may engage in risky sexual behavior, such as having unprotected sex or having sex with multiple partners. During depressive episodes, people with bipolar disorder may experience a decrease in sexual desire and difficulty achieving orgasm.

Substance abuse can also affect sexual functioning. Alcohol and drug use can decrease sexual desire and make it difficult to achieve or maintain an erection. Substance abuse can also lead to risky sexual behavior, such as having sex without a condom or having sex with multiple partners.

It's essential to seek help if you're experiencing mental health conditions that are affecting your sexual functioning. Talking to a healthcare provider or mental health professional is the first step in addressing these issues. Treatment options may include therapy, medication, or a combination of both.

In conclusion, mental health conditions can have a significant impact on sexual functioning. It's crucial to understand how these conditions can affect your sex life and seek help if you're experiencing any difficulties. With the right treatment, it's possible to manage these conditions and improve your sexual satisfaction and overall well-being.

Seeking Help for Sexual and Mental Health Concerns

and "Mental Health".

It is essential for young men to prioritize their sexual and mental health. Sometimes, it can be difficult to seek help for these concerns due to fear, stigma, or embarrassment. However, it is crucial to understand that seeking help is a sign of strength and taking control of one's well-being.

Sexual health concerns can range from sexually transmitted infections (STIs) to erectile dysfunction (ED). If you have experienced any symptoms or have engaged in risky sexual behavior, it is important to get tested for STIs. Many STIs can be treated with antibiotics, but if left untreated, they can lead to serious health complications. ED can also be treated with medication or therapy, but it is important to talk to a healthcare provider to determine the underlying cause.

Mental health concerns can also impact sexual health. Depression, anxiety, and stress can all affect sexual desire and function. It is crucial to seek help for these concerns as well. This can include therapy, medication, or lifestyle changes such as exercise and healthy eating habits.

It can be challenging to talk about sexual and mental health concerns with a healthcare provider, but it is important to remember that they are trained professionals who are there to help. They can provide resources and support to help you navigate these concerns.

In addition to seeking help from a healthcare provider, there are also resources available for young men to learn more about sexual health and mental health. This can include online resources, support groups, and educational programs. By taking the time to educate yourself and seek help when needed, you can prioritize your sexual and mental health and lead a healthy, fulfilling life.

Chapter 8: The Future of Your Sexual Health

Family Planning and Birth Control

and "Reproductive Health"

Family planning and birth control are essential topics for young adult men to understand. It can help them make responsible decisions about their sexual health and prevent unintended pregnancies. In this subchapter, we will discuss the various methods of family planning and birth control available to men.

Condoms are widely recognized as an effective method of birth control. They are easy to use and can prevent the transmission of sexually transmitted infections (STIs). However, it is important to use them correctly and consistently for them to be effective.

Another method of birth control is the withdrawal method, where the man pulls out before ejaculation. While this method can be effective, it is not reliable as it is difficult to predict when ejaculation occurs. Additionally, this method does not provide protection against STIs.

Men can also choose to get a vasectomy, a surgical procedure that involves cutting or blocking the vas deferens, which carries sperm from the testicles to the urethra. This procedure is permanent and is considered a long-term form of birth control.

Hormonal methods of birth control are also available to men. These methods involve the use of testosterone or progestin to suppress the production of sperm. However, these methods are still in the developmental stage and are not yet widely available.

It is important to note that birth control should not be solely the responsibility of women. Men should also take an active role in preventing unintended pregnancies. By understanding the various methods of birth control and family planning, men can make informed decisions about their sexual health.

In conclusion, family planning and birth control are important topics for young adult men to understand. Men should take an active role in preventing unintended pregnancies and protecting themselves from STIs. With the various methods of birth control available, men can make informed decisions about their sexual health.

Fertility and Infertility

Fertility and Infertility

Fertility is the ability to conceive and produce offspring. Infertility, on the other hand, refers to the inability to conceive after a year of regular, unprotected sex. In both cases, it is important to understand the factors that can affect fertility and the steps that can be taken to increase the chances of conceiving.

Factors Affecting Fertility

Age: A woman's fertility declines with age, especially after 35. However, men's fertility also declines with age, although at a slower rate.

Lifestyle factors: Smoking, excessive alcohol consumption, drug use, and obesity can all affect fertility in both men and women.

Medical conditions: Certain medical conditions such as endometriosis, polycystic ovary syndrome (PCOS), and sexually transmitted infections (STIs) can affect fertility in women. In men, conditions such as low testosterone levels, varicocele, and ejaculation problems can affect fertility.

Ways to Increase Fertility

Maintain a healthy lifestyle: Quit smoking, limit alcohol consumption, avoid drug use, and maintain a healthy weight.

Get regular check-ups: Both partners should get regular check-ups to detect and treat any medical conditions that could affect fertility.

Time intercourse: Identify the woman's fertile period (usually around ovulation) and have sex during this time to increase the chances of conception.

Seek professional help: If you have been trying to conceive for a year without success, seek professional help from a fertility specialist.

Infertility Treatments

There are several treatments available for infertility, depending on the cause and severity of the problem. These include:

Medication: This may be used to stimulate ovulation in women or increase sperm count in men.

Intrauterine insemination (IUI): This involves placing sperm directly into the woman's uterus during ovulation.

In vitro fertilization (IVF): This involves collecting eggs from the woman's ovaries and fertilizing them with sperm in a lab. The resulting embryos are then transferred to the woman's uterus.

Conclusion

Fertility and infertility are important topics for young men to understand, especially if they are planning to start a family in the future. By understanding the factors that can affect fertility and taking steps to increase fertility, men can maximize their chances of conceiving. If infertility is a concern, seeking professional help from a fertility specialist can provide valuable guidance and treatment options.

Aging and Sexual Functioning

As men age, their sexual functioning can change, and it is important to understand what to expect. Aging can affect sexual desire, erections, and ejaculation. While these changes are a normal part of aging, they can cause stress and anxiety for some men.

One of the most noticeable changes in sexual functioning is a decrease in sexual desire. This can be due to a decrease in testosterone levels, which is a normal part of aging. It is important to note that a decrease in sexual desire does not mean a decrease in masculinity.

Another change that can occur is difficulty achieving or maintaining an erection. This can be due to a decrease in blood flow to the penis or other health conditions such as diabetes or heart disease. There are treatments available for erectile dysfunction, including medications, vacuum devices, and surgery.

Ejaculation can also be affected by aging. Some men may experience a decrease in the amount of semen produced, while others may have difficulty ejaculating. This can be due to changes in the prostate gland or other health conditions.

It is important to note that sexual functioning can vary greatly from person to person. Just because someone may experience changes in sexual functioning as they age does not mean that they will experience all of the changes discussed above.

Maintaining a healthy lifestyle can help to prevent some of the changes in sexual functioning that may occur with aging. This includes eating a balanced diet, exercising regularly, and managing stress.

It is also important to communicate with sexual partners about any changes in sexual functioning. Open and honest communication can help to alleviate any stress or anxiety that may be associated with these changes.

In conclusion, aging can affect sexual functioning in men. However, there are treatments available to help manage any changes that may occur. Maintaining a healthy lifestyle and communicating with sexual partners can also help to alleviate any stress or anxiety that may be associated with these changes.

Conclusion: Embracing Your Sexual Identity and Enjoying Healthy Sexual Relationships

and "Sexual health."

Conclusion: Embracing Your Sexual Identity and Enjoying Healthy Sexual Relationships

Congratulations! You have made it to the end of this comprehensive guide on sex. You have learned about the anatomy of your body, how to protect yourself from sexually transmitted infections, and how to have enjoyable sexual experiences. However, the most important lesson that you should take away from this book is to embrace your sexual identity and enjoy healthy sexual relationships.

As a young adult man, it is natural to feel confused or uncertain about your sexual orientation or preferences. It is okay to take the time to explore and discover what feels right for you. Remember that sexual identity is a spectrum, and there is no right or wrong way to express yourself sexually. Whether you identify as heterosexual, homosexual, bisexual, or any other label, it is essential to accept and celebrate your unique identity.

Once you have accepted your sexual identity, it is crucial to have healthy sexual relationships. This means being honest with your partner about your desires, using protection to prevent sexually transmitted infections and unwanted pregnancies, and respecting each other's boundaries. Remember that consent is essential in any sexual encounter, and it is never okay to pressure or force someone into doing something they are not comfortable with.

It is also essential to prioritize your sexual health. Regular STI testing, practicing safe sex, and seeking medical attention if you experience any discomfort or unusual symptoms are all crucial steps in maintaining good sexual health. Remember that sexual health is not just about avoiding negative outcomes, but also about experiencing pleasure and satisfaction in your sexual encounters.

In conclusion, embracing your sexual identity and enjoying healthy sexual relationships are essential components of a fulfilling and satisfying life. Remember to always prioritize your sexual health, respect yourself and your partner, and have fun exploring and discovering what feels right for you. With the knowledge and skills you have gained from this guide, you can confidently navigate the world of sex and enjoy all the pleasures it has to offer.

The Ins and Outs of Sex: A Comprehensive Guide for Young Men

Thanks for reading! Best of luck, and happy skill in the art of love & sex.

www.ingramcontent.com/pod-product-compliance
Lightning Source LLC
Chambersburg PA
CBHW071243020426
42333CB00015B/1608